TAKE TEN

TAKE TEN

THE ADULT TIMEOUT FOR THE CREATIVE SOUL

Cynthia Chauvin

with *Miles Chauvin*

TAKE TEN

The Adult Timeout For The Creative Soul

ISBN 13: 978-1-62154-016-8

Cover and Interior Design by Nu-ImageDesign.com

Image Copyright Billdayone, 2012

Used under license from Shutterstock.com

Author photography: Joe Henson

Bebas font courtesy: Ryoichi Tsunekawa

Published by:

Two Dragons International Inc.

Washington D.C. | New Orleans

www.twodragons.com

For special pricing on bulk sales contact

booksales@twodragons.com

For more information and companion audio products please visit

Cynthia's website:

www.cynthiachauvin.com

FOREWORD

My wife Cynthia has done thousands of psychic readings and hypnosis sessions for her clients. The insights in *Take Ten* come from these experiences.

This book and the other books in the *Take Ten* series along with *The 10 Ways*, and our audio CDs are all designed to empower you with the tools to change unproductive thoughts and behaviors.

Whether you use the products together, or separately, the information in each will help you have a better relationship with yourself and others.

Miles Chauvin

INTRODUCTION

E very behavior pattern you have created, started out with a base positive intent to protect you. The behavior may now be antiquated and no longer work to help you, but the intent still holds true.

The power to change these old behaviors lies in your ability to interrupt the patterns in your life and replace them with a broader perspective.

Take Ten was created to be a pattern interrupter, a simple yet effective way to take the moment before an unwanted behavior is repeated and instead fill that moment with insight.

These insights allow you to rethink your present course of action thereby opening you to more choices.

When you see new choices on how to experience a situation, you change your experience. Once an experience is changed, behavior is changed and thereby the outcome changes.

Changes are ecological. When you change one tiny part everything else starts to align itself with that new part. There is no such thing as a small change – it all has a big impact.

HOW TO USE THIS BOOK

The idea is of this book is to literally take ten. When you feel yourself drifting into a sea of depleting, derogatory or unsuccessful repetitive behavior take the book out and think to your self:

"What am I trying to see at this moment? How does this experience want to help me?"

Then flip to a page.

Drink the insight in and let it propagate and inform your thoughts about the situation you are dealing with.

"

The Comfort Zone, unless constantly expanded, first becomes an excuse, second, a trap: and then third, a Hell of our own creation.

"

"

We are meant to be what we already are.

"

"

We are not meant all to sing the same part, we are meant all to sing in harmony.

"

"

I can't commit to non-commitment.

"

"

Perfection has its frailties; that's what makes it perfect.

"

"

Can't love what we judge.

"

"

There is nothing missing from our world, just pieces not yet seen.

"

"

Laughter is good medicine. Laughter at oneself is the nectar of the Gods.

"

"

L ove all of who you are, or you
will never be satisfied.

"

"

When obsession and passion meet the spirit, they open the door to creativity.

"

"

When we pursue, everything runs. When we allow, it just comes.

"

"

D o not bury yourself in your own thoughts. Rise above them and see them, as they are a body of floating information to create from.

"

"

The experience of life is the experience of soul.

"

"

S tand on firm ground; your soul.

"

"

There are thousands of ways to say things, millions of ways to see things, zillions of truths, and one fact-GOD.

"

"

We are all individual books in the library of life.

"

"

If you desire to do something you do it. If you want to do something you do just that-want.

"

"

To inspire life is to see it even in death.

"

"

The viewer sees the world outside in. The thinker sees the world inside out. When the viewer and thinker see each other, then the whole is born.

"

"

Our present state of mind is the present state of consciousness the collective holds. Pass beyond the present state of mind, and discover the universe of creation.

"

"

Wonderment is to knowledge
as wind is to a sail.

"

"

There are no victims in the world, just creators wishing to experience the role of victim.

"

"

At the gateway to Heaven is the acceptance of fear.

"

"

There is an audience for every voice.

"

"

The ego is nothing but scaffolding for the soul to experience the world from.

"

"

Experience is the journey we use to get to our creative power.

"

"

We try so hard to avoid creating any regret that we avoid creating anything new.

"

"

The amazing parts of life speak to us, continually saying there is only One.

"

"

Why do I question what I write today? Because today's wisdoms are tomorrow's limitations.

"

"

Everything is channeled, and everyone is a channeler.

"

"

Rhythm is support to the creative mind.

"

"

Nobody has to tell nature to go to sleep or wake up.

"

"

To create, one must have no direction, no outcome-just discovery.

"

"

We are all in common creation, with individual attitudes about it.

"

"

A quiet mind is always open.

"

"

God has an opinion. They express it all day.

"

"

The only prison is the limitation of the imagination, and we are the jailor.

"

"

You are not an emotion that has a spirit, but a spirit that EXPERIENCES emotions.

"

"

When we succeed in a supportive environment, it is the environment that has succeeded. But when we succeed in the face of adversity, then we have succeeded as a soul, not an ego.

"

"

If you let your emotions live your life, you haven't lived.

"

"

You are a creative part of a collective destiny.

"

"

You are who you look for.

"

"

You can't change the world with a message until the message has changed you.

"

"

Circumstances are only the reflection of our issues.

"

"

We don't pay a price higher than we need because we set the price.

"

"

Creativity is reality, control is just a crayon.

"

"

If you value yourself you will not devalue yourself by another persons actions or thoughts of you.

"

"

The only permanent place is the soul.

"

"

You are never alone just by yourself.

"

"

P urpose causes the mind to focus.

"

"

Fear is the only manipulator in your life.

"

"

Don't let your own expectations keep you from your joy of creativity.

"

"

E verything needs structure to grow.

"

"

I f you know your value you
don't try to prove your value.

"

"

You can't run out of yourself.

"

"

Creativity flows freely when fear of rejection is gone.

"

"

D on't doubt your intuition for someone else's vision.

"

"

Questions are the canvasses of creation.

"

"

Deep vision comes from simple truths.

"

"

We are saved when the mind is no longer an obstruction to the spirit.

"

"

Regret is like paying on a debt you might not even owe.

"

Confusion keeps creativity at bay.

"

"

Compare yourself to everything. Judge yourself by nothing.

,,

"

E verything is a work of art, a masterpiece of life. Brilliant. Perfect. Original. Even our need to repeat and repeat and repeat.

"

"

It is easy to be in your intellect,
but harder to be in your feelings.

"

"

Pierce the veil of reality and you will find yet another reality.

"

"

Everything we know is intuitive. Some of us channel it through our intellect and call it science; some of us channel it through our emotions and call it art.

"

"

The difference between testing faith and having faith is in the attachment to the outcome.

"

"

When we are ready, we experience our creativity instead of experiencing repetition of the same experiences.

"

"

What is discovery but unconscious creation found?

"

Information is gained from books and experience. Wisdom is gained from the soul.

"

"

D on't trust the press. They make something out of nothing and nothing out of something.

"

"

Meeting our destiny has its price, and it is called Faith.

"

"

Extremism is escapism. It is also narcissism.

"

"

When regret enters the door, do not feed it fear anymore-or try to annihilate it, which just creates another regret to take its place. Instead, ask for the grace to see from a different place that which you create.

"

"

Watch with the heart. Hear with the soul. Touch with love. Create from it All.

"

"

E very time you run from, you go to.

"

"

You don't need to judge others to value yourself.

"

"

The purpose of truth is to define a perception.

"

"

All the best things in life can't be explained.

"

"

There is nothing more depressing than a fountain that is not flowing. A person not expressing love is equally sad.

"

"

More root. Less leaf.

"

"

K eep busy lest the mind create mischief.

"

"

E veryone feels helplessness. It's a national past time.

"

"

Truth is simple, when someone tries to make it complex they are trying to hold onto the power it brings.

"

"

Wish for your devils to dance in harmony with your angels.

"

"

The only difference between extremists is what they are extreme about.

"

"

When fear is gone the windows of the mind open freely to the fresh breeze of creativity.

"

"

Instead of preparing for your life, show up for your life and create.

"

"

A writer writes a painter paints a film-maker makes films everyone else just thinks about it.

"

"

There is no information or knowledge that does not come from intuition. We just have different ways in which we access it.

"

"

R hythm is the heartbeat of God.

"

"

The life too examined isn't lived.

"

"

Creativity is thought, word, deed put into action.

"

"

S tructure is a rhythm that supports expression like music and dance.

"

www.ingramcontent.com/pod-product-compliance
Lightning Source LLC
LaVergne TN
LVHW051515080426
835509LV00017B/2071